THE WILDER NONPROFIT FIELD GUIDE TO

Developing Effective Teams

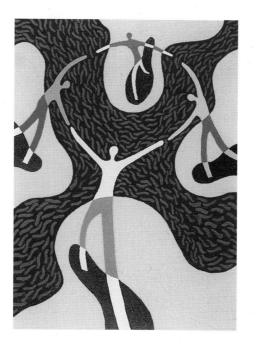

THE WILDER NONPROFIT FIELD GUIDE TO

Developing Effective Teams

Beth Gilbertsen and Vijit Ramchandani

AMHERST H.
WILDER
FOUNDATION

SAINT PAUL,
MINNESOTA

**We thank The David and Lucile Packard Foundation
and the Amherst H. Wilder Foundation for support of this publication.**

The Amherst H. Wilder Foundation is one of the largest and oldest endowed human services and community development organizations in America. For more than ninety years, the Wilder Foundation has been providing health and human services that help children and families grow strong, the elderly age with dignity, and the community grow in its ability to meet its own needs.

The Wilder Nonprofit Field Guide series has been developed by the Wilder Publishing Center to help you and your organization find success with the daily challenges of nonprofit and community work. Other titles in this series include

> *Conducting Successful Focus Groups*
> *Getting Started on the Internet*
> *Fundraising on the Internet*

More titles are in development—to see the latest, please visit our web site at WWW.WILDER.ORG. If you would like to submit an idea or manuscript to the series, please contact us at

> Publishing Center
> Amherst H. Wilder Foundation
> 919 Lafond Avenue
> Saint Paul, MN 55104
> 651-659-6024

Edited by Vincent Hyman
Manufactured in the United States of America
First printing, June 1999

Library of Congress Cataloging-in-Publication Data

Gilbertsen, Beth, date.
        The Wilder nonprofit field guide to developing effective teams /
    Beth Gilbertsen and Vijit Ramchandani.
            p. cm.
        Includes bibliographical references.
        ISBN 0-940069-20-2 (pbk.)
        1. Teams in the workplace. 2. Nonprofit organizations.
    I. Ramchandani, Vijit, date. II. Title.
    HD66.G545   1999
    658.4'02--dc21   99-35048

About the Authors

BETH C. GILBERTSEN has more than twenty years of experience as a facilitator, human resource manager, and training program developer. As owner and principal consultant of CorBridge Learning, Minneapolis, Minnesota, her clients range from small nonprofit organizations to large, multidivisional corporations in electronics, chemicals, food, finance, publishing, telecommunications, industrial products, and medical services. Her expertise includes building teamwork with all levels and types of groups; designing and delivering custom seminars on management, leadership development, conflict resolution, negotiating skills, effective presentation skills, and group and interpersonal communication; and writing guidebooks and curricula.

Beth has served as president of Human Resource Professionals of Minnesota, is a member of the American Society for Training and Development, and is an active volunteer and board member for several organizations. She is a graduate in psychology from Hamline University in St. Paul, Minnesota, and has done graduate work in organizational communications at the University of Minnesota.

VIJIT RAMCHANDANI is a senior consultant with the Amherst H. Wilder Foundation Community Services Group in St. Paul, Minnesota. In this capacity, he manages Wilder's leadership development programs and services, including the Neighborhood Leadership Program and the Southeast Asian Leadership Program for community leaders. As a trainer and consultant, he assists nonprofit organizations, public sector agencies, and Wilder programs with a wide range of organizational development consulting services. He has designed and led a variety of workshops and consulting projects focusing on team building, collaboration, strategic planning, board governance, conflict resolution, cross-cultural effectiveness, and leadership development. Prior to his work at Wilder Foundation, Vijit worked as a senior trainer and organizational development specialist for DataCard and Honeywell corporations.

Vijit is an active volunteer and board member for a variety of community organizations. He is a graduate in psychology and philosophy from Hartwick College, New York, and has done graduate work in intercultural communication at the University of Minnesota.

Acknowledgments

Thanks to a few people who taught me a lot about teamwork and organizational change: Ann Elliott Sterling, Mary Ann Donahue, and Al Van Arsdal. My thanks also to three people who have helped me learn about teamwork, and with whom I have taught many project leadership and teamwork classes: Judy Chayer, Dan Austin, and Jim McCutcheon. Finally, the person who taught me the most has been Don Gilbertsen, not just as a father guiding my youth, but in the early days of my career, when I hadn't a clue where to start.

—Beth Gilbertsen

Thanks to my brother Vivek Ramchandani, who taught me that the essence of good teamwork is believing that two heads are better than one when you're trying to influence a family of four. Thanks also to my tennis coaches, who taught me a lot about what it means to be a team player, and to my colleagues over the past fifteen years as an organization development professional at Honeywell, DataCard, and the Amherst H. Wilder Foundation. Finally, thanks to my lifelong teammate and coauthor, Beth, for always being on my team.

—Vijit Ramchandani

CONTENTS

Why Your Nonprofit Must Learn Teamwork

AS A NONPROFIT LEADER, you have often heard the words *collaboration, partnering,* and *cooperation*. Many funders are beginning to expect these forms of teamwork and often require them. Complex community issues cry out for the cooperation of groups of neighbors, task forces, and board committees. All these situations would benefit from the team approach.

In addition, the multifaceted issues in your work demand multiple perspectives. Because the team approach focuses many minds on an issue, it often yields superior solutions—solutions that are superior in quality and superior because they are devised by the people who will do the work.

Team participation has another benefit: It builds ownership. When both the product and process of teamwork are well tended, people feel deeply satisfied and committed. They know they belong to something bigger than themselves. These feelings are at the heart of why people work and volunteer for nonprofit organizations.

Some would suggest that teamwork is natural to the nonprofit sector. Many nonprofits pride themselves on their egalitarian culture. Their leaders may encourage decisions by consensus, attend to both process and product, and involve clients and constituents in decisions that other types of organizations would consider private. These aspects of the nonprofit culture prepare the workforce for teamwork, but they do not automatically create good teams.

Teamwork is rarely simple, easy, or natural. European cultural values and Western tradition, especially in North America, have rewarded individual work and achievement over the often challenging and unpredictable rhythms of teamwork. Beyond the influences of culture, other problems and barriers can block effective teamwork:

- Unmet or unrealistic expectations
- Resistance by members and people outside the team
- Conflict between members or between teams
- Unclear procedures or ways of doing things
- Role and responsibility confusion
- Ineffective leadership

These types of problems are typical when groups of people try to get something done together, and most work teams should expect to face some of them. Our hope is that this guide assists you in pursuing your team's success, regardless of your role on the team.

Last, when we speak of using the "team approach" or "team concept," we are not referring to a team-building program. Rather, we are talking about an attitude, a preferred way of working when it makes sense. The core belief of this attitude is that two heads are better than one.

Who is this guide for?

Nonprofit organizations and community groups

This guide is intended for any nonprofit, board committee, staff group, community group, or government agency or individual that uses or wants to use the team concept. All types of organizations, including neighborhood groups, volunteers, and board members, will benefit from the tips and processes found here.

Both team leaders and team members who want to improve their teamwork

All teams require planning of and attention to both the "work" and the "working"—also called *task and process* or *product and process*. The *work* means attending to *what* you're working on, the goals and activities. The *working* means attending to *how* you're working on the tasks, the different dynamics a team experiences as it changes through its stages of growth and development.

Temporary or permanent teams

The tips in this guide will help temporary teams (often called project teams), board committees, and special task forces set up to accomplish a task within a limited time frame. These teams are typically accountable to some other outside source or organization. The tips will also help more permanent teams continually improve their effectiveness.

Successful teamwork rarely happens by chance. Leaders and members need to balance the time and energy they devote to working on the task with the time and energy they spend discussing and agreeing on how the work will be done.

How to use this guide

The information, tools, and worksheets that follow are a collection of our best tried-and-true team development techniques. We want you to feel like this is your team's "owner's manual." We hope it helps you get your team started, understand some of the predictable problems that most teams face, and improve your teamwork, regardless of your team's stage of development. Even the best teams struggle with many of the challenges these tools help address.

This guide has four sections:

Section 1, *Understanding Teams,* explains what a team is, how teams grow and develop, and typical barriers teams face.

Section 2, *Tools for Getting Your Team Going,* provides seven tools and techniques for starting your team effort. In addition to their use during team startup, you may return to many of these as ways to keep your team motivated when interest and commitment wanes.

Section 3, *Tools to Keep Your Team Growing,* provides seven tools for strengthening your team while dealing with common team challenges.

The **Appendix** includes an annotated bibliography and worksheets that accompany some of the tools.

Some of the tools might best be initiated by an appointed or informal team leader, but leaders generally want members to take responsibility for effective team functioning. So, no matter what your role is on the team, do whatever you can to use people's time and energy productively. Good luck with your teaming!

Understanding Teams

What Is a Team?

A TEAM IS GENERALLY DEFINED as a group of two or more people who share a common goal and are interdependent in that the tasks necessary to accomplish the goal require them to work together. While there is no agreed-upon "ideal" team size, most teams tend to be comprised of six to eight members. Once the group becomes larger than eight members, the team usually needs to subdivide into smaller groupings to get things done.

The business of working effectively and interdependently to achieve common goals is much easier said than done. Much has been written about effective, productive, high-performing teams. In general, they seem to share the following characteristics:

1. The *goals* and *mission* are
   - Understood by all
   - Committed to by all
   - Viewed as worthwhile and challenging

2. The *roles* are
   - Understood by all
   - Agreed to by all

3. The *procedures* and *processes* are
   - Understood by all
   - Adequately documented
   - Respected and followed

4. The *work environment* and *values* are conducive to
   - Effective working relationships
   - Conflict resolution
   - Exchange of feedback
   - Trust, respect, and recognition
   - Open sharing of information
   - Enjoyment and celebration

5. The team's *leadership* models and creates
   - Commitment and motivation
   - Positive behavior
   - Shared power and leadership through competence
   - Productive meetings

Team Leadership

Jay Conger, assistant professor of organizational behavior at McGill University in Montreal, wrote of leadership, "Most of us have known leaders at work who capture our imagination with a passion for an idea—a vision of the way the future could be. They seem to possess a certain indescribable energy that inspires and motivates. . . . Often we find ourselves, quite willingly, drawn to them."[1]

This is a tall order for the potential team leader. It scares off some excellent candidates before they even attempt taking a leadership role on a team. This expectation is also beyond what's really needed on most teams: While inspired

---

[1] Jay Conger, *The Charismatic Leader,* Jossey-Bass, 1989, page xi.

leadership is a plus, most team leaders are simply solid, well-respected per-
formers who are trusted for their skills and expertise. Good leaders are able to
effectively coordinate and delegate work and create accountability and commitment in each team member.

How people become team leaders

Usually when a team is identified as the best means to get work done, the
management or governing group that convenes the team also designates its
leader. Whether or not this is the best practice, it *is* the most common method
of team leader selection.

Other times, the group that commissions the team may ask that the team select
its own leader. If this is the case, the chosen leader may have more group
support from the onset.

Some teams are allowed the freedom to select their own leaders even though
they are part of a more permanent team, such as a self-managed team. If this is
the case, teams often decide to rotate the leadership responsibility to give
everyone an opportunity to lead and to even out the workload.

Regardless of how team leaders are chosen or how they emerge from the team,
all team leaders have the chance to earn respect and credibility from members—and to lose it.

The role and expectations of team leaders

Team leaders and members should discuss and agree on their expectations of
each other, as well as check and clarify their respective roles and responsibilities. Following are some typical leadership duties:

- *Build commitment and accountability*
  Leaders should ensure objectives and priorities are clear to all team
  members and that members stay focused on goals and key issues.
  Leaders should also assist members when they are pulled in directions
  that do not serve the team's overall mission. Leaders should also plan
  appropriate recognition events and rewards for team performance.

- *Create a positive and motivating atmosphere*

  The leader should be a positive presence on the team. This includes attending team meetings and gatherings, being a spokesperson for the team, and addressing conflict before it becomes destructive.

- *Lead by sharing power and demonstrating competence*

  The leader should recognize that he or she is not the only "expert" on the team. (In fact the whole team concept is about sharing expertise.) Leaders should encourage members to take responsibility and assume authority when needed to accomplish important team tasks inside and outside of the team structure. A mature leader helps the members who are most competent to lead discussions, decisions, and tasks that relate to their expertise, as opposed to keeping a tight rein on members.

- *Conduct productive meetings*

  Leaders should ensure effective and productive meetings. Meetings are a means for reporting information, problem solving, and decision making; they can also be somewhat social and help to build relationships. Leaders should seek to balance these according to the different needs of team members.

While most of this field guide addresses a fictional "team leader," any team member can apply most of the suggestions. Members could make suggestions for improvement during team meetings or consult with the formal leader and offer to help the team out.

When Is a Group a Team?

Teamwork means different things to different people. Not all groups work well as a team, and working as a team is not always necessary or appropriate.

A lot of groups that work together and want to improve their teamwork and interpersonal relations don't exactly share a mutual or common goal, though their goals might be similar or overlapping. Consider a group of employees who each have a goal to support a health education program manager. While their goals are similar, each person actually operates independently. Though they could benefit from sharing resources, talents, expertise, and training, they don't need each other to accomplish their individual goals. Contrast that group with another group assembled to organize and put on a conference for child care providers. These people *do* share a common goal: to hold the conference on a certain date. The team member who organizes the location needs the team member who is responsible for ordering the food and beverages and another who is in charge of scheduling the speakers and arranges for their audiovisual equipment needs.

Figure 1: The Group–Team Continuum shows groups and teams on either end of a continuum, with the degree of interdependence and shared goals increasing as groups move to the right.

Figure 1. The Group–Team Continuum

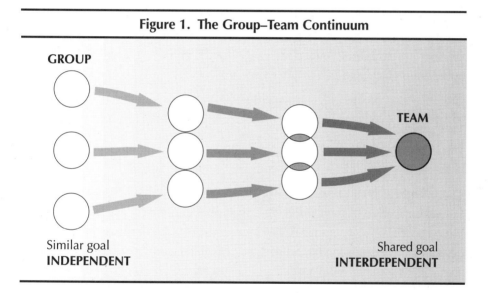

The more a group of people and their work needs move to the right—toward having a common goal—the more teamwork is required of them. When the goal is shared by all, one member's failure to complete a task will usually delay or prevent the achievement of the goal.

The degree to which a group is a team can also be gauged by the extent of interdependence needed among team members to successfully accomplish both individual goals and shared goals. The more the accomplishment of a task requires interdependent behavior from the group of people working toward it, the more that group must function as a team. For example, a group of social workers who work on *separate* cases might benefit greatly from sharing ideas, resources, tips, and approaches, but they can still operate independently and accomplish their goals. In comparison, a multidisciplinary group of mental and physical health care workers who work to help a single client improve his or her situation must operate more interdependently to best use their strengths and avoid duplicating efforts.

Again, the more a group of people and their work requirements move to the right, the more teamwork is needed. The more they must coordinate their work, make efficient handoffs from one member to another, and depend upon one another for successful accomplishment, the more they fit our definition of a team.

Once team members recognize that they need each other to accomplish their shared goal, each member must determine his or her relative contribution toward that goal. The team should develop a plan that combines each team member's contribution toward the goal. (Tool 1, on page 22, will help in developing team plans.)

How Teams Grow

Through research and experience, we know something about how teams grow. Studies have given us models that describe team development and how people behave when working as a team. The models use the idea of group "stages" of development to describe how people's behavior changes over time together.

Each stage has a theme that describes the group activity or overall driving force of the team during that stage of development. This overall driving force is a snapshot of the processes and ways team members relate to each other. These driving forces underlie the work of the team. Sometimes the forces assist team development, and sometimes they do not. It's a mistake to believe that simply because a behavior is predictable, that behavior is necessarily helpful.

The model that follows says that for the team to make progress on its task-related work together, certain group activity must be accomplished and problems resolved at each stage, to a reasonable degree. The model describes broad behaviors that are task related (the work of the group) and relationship oriented (the process of the group). See Figure 2: The Stages of Team Development for a glance at this model.

When reviewing the model, keep in mind

- Each stage is predictable. If the team survives, the theory is that every team will go through each stage.

- Each stage is manageable by the leader. Knowledge of the stages makes effective interventions in the team's activity more predictable and somewhat easier. It offers a plan for leadership.

- Knowledge of the stages helps both the leader and members understand what is happening in the team and why. The model gives a context for diagnosing problems in the team.

Figure 2. The Stages of Team Development

STAGE	GENERAL THEME	TASK GOAL	RELATIONSHIP GOAL
1. Forming	Awareness	Commitment: Becoming oriented	Acceptance: Resolving dependency
2. Storming	Conflict	Clarification: Overcoming resistance	Belonging: Resolving feelings of hostility
3. Norming	Cooperation	Involvement: Promoting open exchange of information	Support: Increasing team cohesion
4. Performing	Productivity	Achievement: Solving problems	Pride: Promoting interdependence
5. Adjourning	Separation	Celebration and closure: Recognizing and documenting team efforts	Satisfaction: Encouraging comments on team performance

The most popular model followed and quoted—and the one we've shown here—was developed by Bruce Tuckman.[2] Tuckman summarized numerous other studies and expressed team stages in short, descriptive, easily remembered

---

[2] Chart and text adapted from B. W. Tuckman, (1965) "Developmental sequence in small groups," *Psychological Bulletin*, 63, p. 384–399 and B. W. Tuckman and M. A. Jensen, (1977) "Stages of small group development revisited," *Group and Organizational Studies*, 2 (4) p. 419–427.

terms. These stages are meant to be descriptive, not prescriptive. As with many theories, it is much easier to reflect in hindsight on how your team moved through these stages; it is difficult to see the stages in action and to plan specific activities to ensure your team develops according to a set of descriptive behaviors. That said, awareness of these developmental stages is an excellent way for members and leaders to know what behaviors might be "normal" and what to encourage (or discourage) while a team is working on its goals and projects.

As you can see in Figure 2, the stages are described as *forming, storming, norming, performing,* and *adjourning.* Following is more information about each stage.

Stage 1: Forming

At the forming stage of team development, members are just coming to know each other and getting used to the idea of working together on a task. To get started on the right foot, members need to learn about, understand, and become committed to the group goals and to be friendly, concerned, and interested in other team members. The desired outcomes for a team in this stage are commitment and member acceptance.

During stage one, team members discover what is acceptable to the group. The stage is characterized by discussions, such as deciding what type of information is needed or talking about problems related to the team goals. Little task-related work is accomplished in the forming stage. Often the awareness of this causes frustration and can yield stage two behaviors (conflict and hostility).

People typically begin with small talk; they get acquainted and discuss their similarities and preferences. Finding one's ground and seeking acceptance is the primary focus for most people at this stage. In many groups in which members feel comfortable with each other, getting acquainted isn't enough. Therefore, the activity that is useful early on is setting mission and goals. This gives meaning to the team's existence.

Tips and tools for FORMING

Here are some actions a team leader can take to help a team during forming:

- Identify potential contributions of team members.

- Spend adequate time on introductions.

- Allow time for people to reveal why they are interested in being part of the group.

- Encourage each person to talk.

- Be a role model for open behavior.

- Be organized and ready to answer questions about what the team is supposed to be doing.

- Know the task, mission, and goals, especially if the task is set by some manager or group other than the team.

- Define and agree on individual roles team members will play to get the task done.

- Ask for and discuss, as a team, people's concerns and questions.

- Be a little more directive in style as a team leader during forming; the team needs more direction at this stage.

Tool 1: Writing a Team Mission Statement (page 22), Tool 2: Setting Team Goals (page 24), and Tool 4: Creating Ground Rules to Manage Team Dynamics (page 27) are especially helpful during forming.

Stage 2: Storming

At this stage, conflict emerges naturally as a theme. The conflict may be about mission, goals, other members, and leadership, as members begin to question the assumptions that underlie the team charter and find ways to demonstrate resistance. They can become hostile or overzealous as a way to express their individuality. Other group expressions of this stage are polite disagreements, fake agreements, infighting, defensiveness, and competition. During this stage, little task-related work is accomplished. Members are adjusting to each other and shifting their perspectives from those of individuals to those of team member. Team members seek clarification and a sense of belonging during this stage.

At all times during teamwork, but especially during the storming stage, leaders should seek to develop an atmosphere that encourages and supports the open expression of diverse points of view. Members should try to listen attentively and actively to all perspectives. The diversity of shared opinions provides the team with a vital source of group energy and also often leads to conflict between one or more members or between factions within the group. By openly confronting and managing disagreements, a team clarifies its purpose and begins to define effective ways for working together on a deeper level.

Tips and tools for STORMING

Here are some actions a team leader can take to help a team during storming:

- Watch for fight, flight, or submission. Of the three, try to encourage direct conflict ("fight"), because it is easier to manage in the long run.

- Draw all members into the conversation.

- Seek opposing views.

- Listen carefully.

- Clarify and paraphrase positions.

- Summarize to determine areas of agreement.

- Help conversations move along.

- Watch for noncontributing team members; talk to them after team meetings to find out why they aren't contributing.

- Be a role model for openness.

- Be able to clarify the team's mission, tasks, and goals.

- Raise questions you think other team members might be thinking.

- Allow for compromise.

- Focus on areas in which team members agree, at least in principle.

- Seek to resolve personal concerns and issues affecting the life of the team.

- Gently confront team member conflicts and try to openly discuss differences.

- Generate more options to problem solving.

- Use a coaching style of leadership.

Tool 10: Resolving Conflict within a Team (page 39) can be helpful during Storming. To help during conflict discussions, revisit the results from Tool 4: Creating Ground Rules to Manage Team Dynamics (page 27).

Stage 3: Norming

The norming stage has an overall theme of cooperation and is characterized by attempts to achieve maximum harmony by collectively *avoiding* conflict. It is the calm after the storm. Once a team has moved through stage two, members have found a way to manage their own conflicts and frequently do not wish to return to stage two behavior. They want to do what they can to create a feeling of "team-ness." Members begin to accept the team's ground rules and each others' idiosyncrasies. They see that the chance for team success increases as they share power and resources.

There is an atmosphere of trust, support, and cooperation. Members confide in each other, share personal and team problems, and focus their attention on improving team dynamics. Members seem to be able to express emotions and ideas more constructively. As all these dynamics play out, the team also accomplishes a moderate amount of its assigned work.

Team cohesion becomes a team norm, and a feeling of genuine support develops. Members learn that to work together effectively, they must learn to be honest when giving and receiving feedback. The leader, in this stage, can typically rely more on members for accomplishing tasks and making progress than in earlier stages of the team's life.

Tips and tools for NORMING

Here are some actions a team leader can take to help a team during norming:

- Watch for conflict avoidance or agreement for the sake of agreement.

- Confront conflict in private.

- Check in with members individually to get viewpoints that may not be reflected in the group; remember that individuals behave differently when influenced by the group.

- Give rewards and recognition to encourage task accomplishment.

- Have accurate, up-to-date information on external conditions affecting the work of the team.

- Use a supporting, nondirective leadership style.

To ensure members' work is progressing, use Tool 14: Communicating between Meetings (page 46) to be sure that communication channels are working. Revisit Tool 6: Creating Team Project Plans (page 32) to be sure that the plan the team made continues to be useful.

Stage 4: Performing

During this stage of development, the general theme is productivity. Team members direct their energy toward solving problems and promoting interdependence. Leaders encourage everyone to contribute ideas, and problems are resolved cooperatively.

During the performing stage members work to their greatest potential to achieve desired goals and objectives, and a great deal of work is accomplished. In fact, a major challenge for leaders is sustaining momentum and motivation. Leaders can use the milestones achieved or established benchmarks to revitalize the team and capitalize on the intrinsic rewards members receive by being productive.

When the team is truly performing, the team feels a sense of pride. They celebrate both individual and group achievements. In contrast, during the three previous stages, celebrating individual achievement might work against the developing sense of teamwork. At the performing stage, however, the team is mature enough to appreciate each other and the fruits of their labor together.

Tips and tools for PERFORMING

Here are some actions a team leader can take to help a team during performing:

- Continue one-on-one contact to accurately assess whether team members feel like they are accomplishing their tasks effectively.

- Frequently celebrate, reward, and recognize each other's progress and contributions to task accomplishment.

- See balance between individual recognition and team recognition.

- Look for opportunities to give the team visibility.

- Don't avoid conflict; bring it up and discuss it openly.

- Use a delegating leadership style.

Teams that want help understanding their own success can use Tool 9: Assessing Overall Team Effectiveness (page 39). This tool may help the team feel successful even as the team fine-tunes itself. Teams that are working well together usually strive, on their own, to improve and maintain successful task accomplishment. In this sense, no tool is really needed. Teams can revisit any of the tools at any time to tune up performance, however.

Stage Five: Adjourning

The adjourning stage of team development may occur for teams that have a predetermined lifetime, as in time-specific committees and task forces. It may also occur when a major task is completed or when a number of new team members are added or changed. Some ongoing teams do not conclude at the fifth stage, but recycle from stage four to stage one without adjourning.

For teams that are adjourning, an evaluation of team accomplishments provides important feedback that can be used to plan future ventures involving other teams or groups. It also provides a sense of closure for the team members and allows members to say good-bye or to commit to a future of further teamwork or collaboration.

Tips and tools for ADJOURNING

The goal in adjourning is to formally close the team's work in a way that celebrates both individual and team success. Here are some elements of a successful ending ritual:

- Choose a time and place where the team members can all be present.

- Talk about what each person contributed to the team.

- If appropriate, involve some of the people affected by the team.

- Tell some stories about the team's work together.

- Choose some activities that everyone enjoys.

We offer no specific tools for adjourning. This is the time to encourage team members to celebrate, reflect, and renew. The team is best able to plan its own adjourning event.

These stages do not occur for every team, nor do they always occur in the noted order. But as unpredictable as human beings are, they do sometimes behave in a textbook fashion. On the other hand, teams of people can do strange things.

Because the forming, storming, and norming stages are not always productive times for the team, it is tempting to try and find ways to rush through or short-circuit the stages in hopes of achieving your team's goals faster. Although the idea is seductive, experiencing the different stages in some form is inevitable. Just as individuals go through childhood, adolescence, young adulthood, midlife, and old age, teams go through predictable stages. A team that knows what to expect during each stage will ride the waves of each stage and continue functioning productively.

Common Barriers to Teamwork

There are a host of typical barriers to effective teamwork, many related to stages of development, that all teams must overcome to be successful. Some teams succeed in spite of these barriers. Barriers can stem from problems inside the team, in which case members may have more control over the solutions to these problems. Barriers can also come from outside the team.

Barriers inside the team can include individual egos, achievement drives, apathy, indifference, and members who are unwillingly assigned to the team and believe their talents could be used better elsewhere. Members also come with hidden agendas, baggage, reputations, and special interests. Some members may have unresolved conflicts from previous associations. Members may disagree about roles, goals, missions, membership, and leadership, and they may have no interest in addressing these problems.

Barriers outside the team include limited or diminishing resources, languishing support systems and structures, unclear goals and mission requirements, competing priorities, contradictory messages, imposed competition, waning support from stakeholders or constituents, and an organizational culture characterized by tight management control in which teams have no real authority to make decisions.

The tools in this field guide help prevent the occurrence of some of these barriers. However, many events and barriers emerge that do not respond to any one technique, process, or activity. Typically, you need to deploy a combination of strategies to eliminate or minimize the impact of a particular barrier.

Changes in Team Membership and Leadership

Teams sometimes undergo changes in membership, as members change employment, certain tasks end, and so forth. Less often, a team will change leaders (except in cases where teams appoint their own regularly changing leader).

When a new team member comes on board, it feels a little like minor surgery. The new member will ask questions the team thinks it has already answered, and some team members can grow impatient. Often the team has to revisit some earlier stages in its development. This takes time but is unavoidable.

To help ease the discomfort of the situation

- Take time for introductions and point out each team member's role and specialty.
- Revisit the team goals and mission.

- Orient new members to the team's existing way of doing things—who does what, written and unwritten rules, and so forth.

- Share the team's history, "war stories," and inside jokes.

- Ask new members for their suggestions and needs in terms of how the team functions, and adapt the team's rules and norms accordingly. Don't force the new team member to conform to the status quo.

The introduction of a new team leader, especially from outside the team, will feel like major surgery. Team members will be confused, and most team members will feel like they are starting over, especially if the new leader's style differs from that of the outgoing leader. The suggestions for adding a new team member also apply to adding a new team leader. The team and leader can develop a plan to help ease the transition. Although it may feel awkward, strong team members should help orient the new team leader.

Sustaining a Long-Lived Team

When people work together for a sustained period of time, they begin to accept each other, which is not the same as agreeing with or liking each other's attributes. Such acceptance seems to occur whether member characteristics or working styles are perceived as strengths or liabilities to teamwork. Effective teams are able to use helpful characteristics and attributes for the benefit of the team and to minimize member liabilities.

As a practical matter, long-lived teams are almost always in a state of flux. Members and leaders come and go, creating opportunities to reset direction and clarify roles. To be sure, too much attention to team dynamics may make members feel as though they are spinning their wheels and not making progress on important goals and plans. Nevertheless, changes in team composition require revisiting some of the basic tasks of team development, as described in the previous section.

Regardless of changes in team composition, long-running teams can usually benefit from revisiting their mission and goals (Tool 1 and Tool 2), renegotiating roles (Tool 12), and updating project plans (Tool 6). Durable teams often face funding changes, and funders want to review strategic planning documents or long-term plans of where the team is going with its resources. This chance to do future planning can energize a team and help refocus their efforts and relationships; Tool 7: Developing Team Spirit, can be useful at this point. Other long-lived teams might benefit from planning discussions of their meeting effectiveness (Tool 8) and overall team effectiveness (Tool 9) as a way to sustain their teamwork, stay motivated, and continually improve.

In our experience, effective and durable teams build themselves continuously by attending equally to getting their work done (they focus on task accomplishment) and to how well they do the work (they reflect on their group process and plan for improvements in it). This balancing act contributes to a thriving, sustained team effort.

With patience, persistence, and a potent kind of caring, most groups of people who want to become an effective team can do so.

Summary

This section provided you with a definition of how a team differs from a group and what typically characterizes an effective team. We also reviewed how teams develop and mature over time and some other aspects of teams. Our aim is simple: to provide you with a model of team development to help you respond to team problems and barriers.

A final note: We have observed (and experienced ourselves) that some teams that face countless obstacles still have a positive energy or chemistry that carries the team onward to success. Where this chemistry comes from exactly, or how to achieve it deliberately, is a compelling question practitioners like us ponder. Some people have compared it to the magic that emerges when jazz musicians "get in the groove." Other phrases you'll hear to describe this chemistry are "synergy" and "like a well-oiled machine." These images can lead one to believe that true teamwork is rarely obtained. We believe that with patience, persistence, and a potent kind of caring, most groups of people who want to become an effective team can do so. All they need is a few tools and a road map.

Tools for Getting Your Team Going

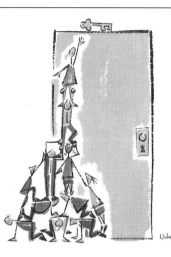

THE TOOLS IN THIS SECTION can help you or key members get your team started on the right track. These tools are

- Tool 1:   Writing a Team Mission Statement
- Tool 2:   Setting Team Goals
- Tool 3:   Conducting Effective Team Meetings
- Tool 4:   Creating Ground Rules to Manage Team Dynamics
- Tool 5:   Decision Making in Teams
- Tool 6:   Creating Team Project Plans
- Tool 7:   Developing Team Spirit

These tools don't have to be used in any order, but they all center around important tasks during the early stages of team formation. Though team members are often willing to jump into working on the issues and getting things done, they also need to define their mission and goals and clarify how meetings and decisions will be made. Tools 1 through 5 can help them accomplish these important procedural tasks.

The tool for team planning (Tool 6) helps involve the whole team in developing a work plan, which is important when the schedule is tight and work must be done in parallel. An additional benefit of such planning is that it helps team members start their work together by using personal expertise and with a feeling of personal relevance, which eventually gives rise to a sense of shared ownership and commitment.

The seventh tool in this section, Developing Team Spirit, provides a variety of ideas to cement working relationships on your team and increase team cohesion.

Tool 1: Writing a Team Mission Statement

A team's mission statement defines the team's purpose or reason for existing. It describes key goals, shared values, who the team serves, and what difference the team intends to make. It is the foundation on which the team's house is built.

Team mission statements help

- Provide a context for decision making. When a situation is unclear, team members can refer to their mission as a guide to action.

- Provide a focus for collaboration and shared responsibility. Coordination within a team can be difficult when there is not a clear and shared mission.

- Move the team toward excellence and high performance. Powerful missions can inspire people to go above and beyond what they are expected to achieve because they recognize what they are working toward.

Teams often define their mission in the early stages of coming together. But a mission is seldom static, even though it provides the team's basic focus and foundation. We recommend that teams engage in periodic reviews and revisions of their mission as conditions change in and around the team.

How to write a mission statement

Convene the team to discuss the points listed below. Encourage participation by all members. Additional input might be solicited from people or sources outside the team—for example, leaders and other stakeholders, clients, colleagues, and community members.

Use Worksheet A: Writing a Team Mission Statement *on page 53 to create your team's mission statement.*

1. Find a *reference point and an anchor* for your team's mission. The reference point usually comes from the larger entity in which the team is embedded or to whom it is responsible. Does your community, department, work group, or agency have a mission statement or vision? Use this as a reference point to align your team's work. For example, if a team within a family services agency wants to establish a home-based service, a possible reference point would be the overall mission statement for the agency.

2. Given the larger mission and goals that your team serves, what is the *purpose* of your team? Using the example above, the team might decide its purpose is to get the home-based service defined, staffed, and running within six months.

3. Encourage each team member to do the following:

   a) Define the team's *products, services, results,* or *outcomes.* For example, a team member from the home-based family services team wrote, "We offer client home care, we help reduce family stress, we help family functioning, and we are cost-effective."

   b) Identify the team's *audiences, customers, clients,* or *stakeholders.* Continuing the example, the team member wrote, "Our clients are elderly people with no transportation, past clients, and current clients who have a hard time making it to our location."

   c) Determine what *needs* and *functions* the team serves. Continuing, another team member wrote, "We fill needs for physical therapy, basic family education about aging, basic nursing care, problem solving, and the need to be listened to and supported."

   d) Identify the *values* or *standards* that guide the team's work or characterize the team's "culture." Team members identified these team values: "respect for privacy, kindness, compliance with regulations, responsiveness, and well-trained staff."

4. Ask a subteam (two to three people) to combine the points discussed and to write one or more draft mission statements to present to the entire team. Continuing with the same example, the first draft of the team's mission statement read, "Our team's mission is to develop and provide a responsive, caring, professional, and cost-effective home-based health care service to aid the physical and mental well-being of our clients."

5. After reviewing the draft mission statement(s), draft a final statement incorporating revisions.

6. Align goals and work plans to fit the mission.

7. Communicate the mission statement to key stakeholders and others as appropriate.

8. Review the mission periodically and align current goals or revise the mission to fit changed circumstances. Also use the team mission as a guide to help determine priorities and make key decisions.

Tool 2: Setting Team Goals

Goal setting gives your team direction and, as goals are achieved, gives you a measure of progress. Goals differ from a mission in that they are more specific, are often measurable, and have a deadline. They also may relate to a certain program or service. The team as a whole might have goals, and members might also have their own goals.

Goals are useful because they

- Focus work on measurable outcomes
- Translate the team's mission into specific tasks
- Attach specific tasks to the team mission or charter
- Help evaluate progress and effectiveness
- Help establish priorities among conflicting demands
- Express standards and expectations for performance and learning

Goals respond to the essential question, "Where are we going?" Often groups have an overall goal and then specific goals and related tasks followed by strategies and steps to achieve each goal. Both overarching and specific goals are important and need to be understood and endorsed by all team members.

When teams get into trouble, one of the first places to check is the team's goals. Poor performance may stem from indifference to or lack of clarity about team goals.

Use input from the board, staff, clients, volunteers, and other key stakeholders when setting goals, but be sure the team decides exactly what it wants to accomplish. That way, the team "owns" the goals and shares responsibility for accomplishing them.

How to set team goals

1. Review tasks and goals that already exist, such as program goals, department goals, and past accomplishments. Identify and select areas where the team would like to set goals. If the team has existed for a while, identify where members would like to clarify, revise, and improve existing goals.

2. Brainstorm possible goals directed at helping your team move ahead toward your mission.

3. Discuss your ideas for goals. Are they realistic? Achievable? Does the team have the resources and ability to get the job done? What are reasonable measures or criteria for success? For example, a realistic goal for the agency developing a new home-based elderly service might be "Write a communications plan and brochure to let existing and potential clients learn about our services by June 1."

4. Prioritize the goals according to the criteria for success and other considerations discussed in point 3 above.

5. Agree on specific dates for when goals should be completed and when progress should be reviewed.

Once the team has set goals, they need to move quickly toward accomplishing them. This is often best done by dividing up labor and responsibilities for implementation. Ask individuals or subteams to make more detailed plans and determine who will do what and when they will do it.

Tool 3: Conducting Effective Team Meetings

Meetings are often the primary forum for members to get acquainted, exchange information, report on activities, and discuss and resolve issues. For many people, the team meeting is what they identify with or visualize when they think of their team.

Meeting frequency depends on the goals, tasks, and activity levels of team members. If members require a lot of interdependence and their goals overlap greatly, more frequent meetings are necessary, and they will usually focus on information exchange, problem solving, and decision making.

The following tips are concrete steps you can take toward having productive meetings. In general, effective meetings depend on five key things:

1. Distributing agendas in advance

2. Starting and stopping on time

3. Using time efficiently

4. Leaving each meeting with next steps in place

5. Following through on decisions

Tips for meeting preparation

- Ask all team members for ideas and issues to be included in the meeting agenda.

- Distribute the agenda ahead of time.

- Ask all team members to come prepared with their comments and suggestions to use meeting time efficiently.

Tips for conducting team meetings

- Aim to start and end the meetings on time.

- To achieve balanced participation, draw out quieter members for their comments and gently and respectfully direct the group's attention away from those who are dominating the discussion.

- Use the agenda as a discussion guide. Some of the team members' tangents might be useful to your meeting and some might not. Encourage members to speak up if the discussion isn't useful to them.

- Near the end of the meeting, recap and summarize key points and decisions and decide on next steps.

- Determine individual roles and responsibilities to carry out next steps and other expectations.

Tips for meeting follow-up

- Publish and distribute minutes or meeting notes.

- Complete actions that you agreed to carry out.

- Report progress to the rest of the team, as agreed.

Tool 4: Creating Ground Rules to Manage Team Dynamics

What is happening between and to team members while the team is working directly affects how well the team functions. Sensitivity to human needs for power, achievement, and inclusion, as well as to differing values, cultural backgrounds, experience levels, and influence styles, allows leaders and members to better manage discussions, to diagnose team problems early, and to deal with them more effectively.

Having and using norms or ground rules can help manage the behavior of group members both during and between team meetings. Norms usually express the beliefs or desires of the majority of the team and make explicit the behaviors that should or should not take place in team interactions.

Some norms are clear, explicit, and known, and some norms are implicit and sensed by only a few. Some norms facilitate group progress and some hinder it. For example, an explicit norm that might help the team is *During team meetings we will avoid side conversations.* An implicit norm that might hinder the team is *Members who speak out the most often get their way.*

One of the best ways to effectively manage dynamics is to discuss and establish group norms or ground rules that focus on how members are expected to behave and interact toward other team members. Sometimes teams develop these before they start their work together as a prevention mechanism, and sometimes the ground rules are developed as needed. For example, if the team runs into a problem, they might stop and discuss how they want to handle it according to their ground rules.

Team ground rules help

- Express the values and desires of team members
- Make sure every team member knows and agrees with what's expected of him or her
- Support the needs of the team and reflect the culture of the agency or community
- Evaluate team performance
- Orient new members to team expectations of "how things are done around here"

Here are some common team dynamics for which explicit ground rules can be established:

- Participation
- Work-related conflicts and disagreements
- Personal conflicts, needs, and issues
- Ways in which decisions will be made
- Confidentiality
- Leadership roles and responsibilities
- Communication practices
- Feedback and criticism
- Rewards and recognition

Here are the ground rules one team developed to guide their team meetings:

1. Members are responsible for stating what they want from team meetings when their needs differ from the usual agenda.

2. There will be no side conversations.

3. All views will be heard before a team decision is made.

4. Two-thirds of the members constitute a decision-making body.

5. Competence and experience leads the discussion.

6. Work-related conflicts will be discussed within the team meetings.

7. Personal conflicts between members will be discussed and resolved outside team meetings.

Note: Sometimes teams agree, either implicitly or explicitly, to dysfunctional norms. An example of such a norm is the one cited above: *Members who speak out most often get their way.* If you are working in a team with unhealthy team norms, we suggest your team use Tool 8: Improving Your Team Meetings, page 38, or Tool 9: Assessing Overall Team Performance, page 39, to surface and correct such norms.

How to create ground rules

1. Ask members to think of the teams they have been on that have been effective and what made those teams successful. Discuss all ideas.

2. Decide together which of those characteristics members want to use for their team.

3. Make a written list of the ground rules the team decides would be useful.

4. As the team works together, all members should use these ground rules as a guide for their behavior and interactions with others.

5. When new members join, explain the team's ground rules.
    If many new members join, ground rules may need to be rewritten.

6. Periodically, or annually, the team should evaluate the effectiveness of their ground rules and revise them as needed.

Use Worksheet B: Establishing Team Ground Rules *on page 55 to assist your discussion.*

Tool 5: Decision Making in Teams

Decisions teams make usually have a big impact on the success and effectiveness of the team. Some decision-making styles alienate members, and other styles are not suited to the particular decision being made. When choosing a decision-making style, consider these two criteria for sound decisions:

QUALITY. The decision is logically sound and makes good sense based on the best information available.

ACCEPTANCE. The decision is understood and agreed to by those who must carry it out.

A good decision balances quality and acceptance. It is logical, based on the best information available, and understood and agreed to by the people who must carry it out.

There are many different decision-making methods or styles used by groups and teams. The relative advantages and disadvantages of each depends on the situation and the degree of quality and acceptance needed to make a good decision.

Many teams get comfortable with using one primary method for making decisions and fail to recognize that it is not suited to all situations. For example, the board of directors of a neighborhood block club used voting or "majority rules" for all their decision making. Eventually certain members who were often in the minority left the board of directors because they felt they weren't being heard. Nothing was wrong with the decision-making method itself, but exclusive use of voting was a mistake. Had the board worked to reach consensus on a number of decisions, the "losing" board members would have felt that their positions were valued and acted on. Fewer decisions would have been put to a vote, creating fewer opportunities for winners and losers.

On a team, it is best to decide who should be involved with making particular decisions and which decision-making methods best fit the situation. This also frequently prevents potential conflict, resistance, and misunderstandings that may crop up after the decision has been implemented. We recommend that the team leader opt for the most participatory decision-making process that time allows.

How to choose a decision-making method

1. Determine as a team what process to follow when decisions need to be made. Discuss
   - Who needs to support the decision.
   - Who wants to give input.
   - Whose input is required.
   - Who should make the decision; who has the power.
   - Who will be impacted by the decision.

2. Determine if the decision needs to be made by an individual, the entire team, or a subgroup of the team and which of the decision-making methods described below is the best way to make it.

3. Most team decisions can be *consensus-based, democratic,* or *delegated.* If the team or a subset of the team would be better for the decision, choose either a consensus-based or democratic decision-making style. If an individual is better suited to making the decision, the group leader or team can delegate the decision to that person.

   Consensus-based. This is a decision that everyone can "live with." It is also known as the "win-win" method, in that everyone wins if everyone can live with the decision. Consensus evolves from sharing information and ideas within the group. People who disagree are encouraged to express themselves, not to be quiet. This encourages the group to thoroughly examine whether everyone can truly live with and support the proposed decision, even if there was some disagreement over it. A consensus-based decision, therefore, is *not* a unanimous decision. It is not achieved by voting.

   While consensus is often the most popular and preferred method for making decisions, it is not always the best way to proceed. It takes a lot more time to make the decision and requires skilled communication, active listening, and patience.

Democratic. This is a decision made by voting; the majority vote rules. This is frequently the fallback method when a consensus-based process runs out of time or energy. For this reason, a democratic decision is sometimes referred to as *practical consensus.* When teams vote, there are "winners" and "losers" as compared to the win-win outcome of consensus.

Delegated. This is a decision made by granting someone full authority to decide and asking him or her to let the team or team leader know what was decided. Use this method when a particular member has the experience, special expertise, or background to make the decision, while others lack these attributes. The person might decide *unilaterally,* with little or no influence and input from others, or *consultatively,* by seeking advice from others.

4. Make the decision.

5. Evaluate the effectiveness of the decision, results achieved, and the appropriateness of the decision-making method.

Tool 6: Creating Team Project Plans

Once your team clarifies its mission and goals, members sometimes want a clear plan for how to reach their goals. There are many benefits to talking out and working through the scope and depth of the work to be done. Collectively writing the work plan can help your team flesh out details, clarify or narrow goals, clarify roles and responsibilities, list concerns and assumptions, and list resources needed.

All team members should convene to develop the work plan. Often it's useful to start by restating goals and priorities to be sure that everyone agrees on and understands them. The team should identify the major milestones and steps needed from the beginning of the project all the way to the end.

Teams that have specific projects with start and stop times may find this process more useful than a department or work unit that has ongoing goals and objectives.

How to make a project plan

1. Bring together the entire team and clarify the goals, identify concerns, agree on basic assumptions, and review the resources available.

2. Brainstorm milestones (such as major approvals from upper management or stages of the task) plus all the specific steps members feel are necessary to complete or reach the goal. The steps can be as detailed as individual members want to make them. It's useful, however, to agree on the general level of specificity so people are consistent in their thinking.

3. Using removable stick-on notes, place the milestones in a logical order and then place the steps between them. Remember some steps can be done in parallel, while others must be done sequentially. Tape some paper to a wall and move the stick-on notes around until the plan looks right. Write each milestone on a separate note, and then ask people to reposition it as they discuss the most effective and efficient order.

4. For each of the specific steps, estimate the time needed to complete the step or task, and make a list of resources needed. This activity prevents surprises once work has begun. While listing resources, it's handy to keep a list of concerns and assumptions you are making so all team members are aware of them.

5. If the project has many intricate steps, it may help to draw arrows between steps to indicate the exact order of each step.

6. Team members should write their names or initials on each of the stick-on notes for the tasks that suit them best. These are, in effect, the roles and responsibilities for team members. This way, each team member knows what is expected from all other team members. Plus, each member finds out where his or her work comes from and to whom it should go upon completion.

7. One person should list tasks, time, resources needed, and accountabilities and distribute the list to all members. (Some teams use project-management software for this.)

8. If the timeline is too long, the team should reconvene and see what tasks can be eliminated, shortened, or done in parallel. This is not a disadvantage, however, because the onset of a project is the best time to discover that more human and financial resources will be needed to complete the project. It is better to learn this early in the project than halfway through it!

9. Once the project plan is completed, look over it and think of any other tasks you may add. These might include
   - Formal or informal reviews requested by other organizations or groups
   - Status reports required or requested by others
   - Team celebrations and times for reflection
   - Team-building retreats or review meetings
   - Vacations, leaves of absence, holidays, busy seasons, and other time delays
   - Grant-writing wait periods

Tool 7: Developing Team Spirit

Most teams want to be successful at both accomplishing goals *and* working effectively together. While members don't have to be best friends, it's generally more enjoyable to get acquainted so the team can benefit from each person's unique strengths and expertise.

The following tips to develop team spirit and cohesiveness are ideas both leaders and team members may suggest or initiate at any time in the team's life.

Tips to help individuals feel like a part of a team and improve team spirit

- Have the team create or identify its unique characteristics—a team name, logo, symbol, or their own space with which to identify. For example, one team that met above an import store began calling itself "the team from the global village."

Another team decided to have a T-shirt made with their team logo. They all decided to wear their shirts the day they recruited new volunteers. While the T-shirts and logo set them apart from the potential volunteers, it brought them together as a team. Then, as volunteers came forward, they each were given a T-shirt as a symbol of their joining the larger team.

Another team, created by three organizations that formed a collaborative, designed a banner that incorporated elements of each organization.

- Encourage team members to explore, understand, and appreciate their personal and cultural similarities and differences. For example, schedule times for individuals to tell their stories and talk about their cultures and the communities they belong to, in addition to finding ways to share favorite foods over scheduled staff lunches.

- Situate people within easy reach of one another. As much as possible, locate team members' offices or work areas together. If this is not possible, have a standard meeting place or name your meeting room. Call it "the think tank" or something else descriptive of the team and its work.

- Encourage team members to get to know one another, socialize, and depend on one another. These actions foster team loyalty. Focus on ways people can support and assist each other personally and professionally.

- Help each member identify personal or career development needs that might be met by being part of the team. These might include increased opportunities for recognition, learning, challenge, growth, leadership, and influence.

- Help people see how their team's goals are contributing to the communities they serve. Some people are very motivated by feeling that they have contributed to a larger goal.

- Recognize contributions during and after team interactions—refer to *specific* behaviors you think are useful and helpful to the team's work. That way, team members know what actions help teamwork.

- Find creative ways to recognize, reward, and emphasize the collective skills and strengths of the team overall. For example, surprise the team with a celebration instead of the usual team meeting after the team reaches a major milestone. Celebrate the completion of challenging team tasks.

- Applaud people who step in and go the extra mile. Some members enjoy going beyond the call of duty if they volunteer to do so. One team member thought it would be more efficient if he proofread the final report of his team's project instead of having several proofreaders—and he gave his reasons for that. He stayed up most of the night to do it and said he enjoyed the tight deadline and making the sacrifice for the team. (Make sure you don't go overboard on this.)

- Encourage members to assume complete ownership and responsibility for their jobs. People tend to support what they help create. Coach people to solve their own problems and make their own decisions, especially when they want the leader to make the decision for them. Team members may resist the sudden autonomy that empowerment brings, but it will go a long way toward building a stronger team.

- Show your personal commitment to the team. Honor your own commitment to the team's goals and mission. Your sincerity has a way of being contagious. Formal speeches and slogans can inspire some, but others must feel, touch, and hear personal sincerity at close range.

SECTION 3

Tools to Keep Your Team Growing

THE TOOLS IN THIS SECTION can help you or key members keep the team growing over time. These tools are

Tool 8:   Improving Your Team Meetings
Tool 9:   Assessing Overall Team Effectiveness
Tool 10: Resolving Conflict within a Team
Tool 11: Managing Conflict between Two Teams
Tool 12: Clarifying Roles and Responsibilities
Tool 13: Dealing with Performance Problems
Tool 14: Communicating between Meetings

All teams change and grow over time. The object in teamwork is to continually benefit from it, not make more work for yourself. Keeping a team growing in a productive fashion means tending to members' needs as they change over time, resolving conflicts as they come up, improving individual performance, and building overall team effectiveness.

This section will help team leaders and members with ideas and processes to address conflicts or problems that arise in the course of the teams' life. Goals, plans, roles, priorities, interests, and commitments all have a way of changing and evolving as time goes on. New issues emerge even as commitment and enthusiasm ebb and flow. These tools will help you approach a challenging team dilemma in a systematic and productive way.

Use Worksheet C: Team Meeting Critique Sheet, *on page 57 to assist you with improving your team meetings.*

Tool 8: Improving Your Team Meetings

Meetings are the primary vehicle team members use to discuss problems, challenges, new ideas, and progress on individual work. Most people want meetings to be short, organized, focused, and comfortable. Poorly managed meetings can become unproductive, boring, too long, dominated by one or two stronger personalities, and basically, a miserable waste of time. Over time, regularly scheduled meetings with the same team may become gradually less productive. Addressing these challenges is often tough and time consuming in itself. Periodically, team members might want to take the "temperature" of their meetings and develop ways to have better meetings.

How to improve team meetings

Allow thirty minutes on the agenda to discuss meeting effectiveness.

1. Brainstorm and list characteristics of effective team meetings.

2. Identify those aspects of the meeting (meetings in general or yours) that typically go well—what does your team do well in meetings?

3. Identify those aspects that require improvement in your team meetings. Identify and focus on the two or three highest priority aspects. To help the discussion, use Worksheet C.

4. Agree on a plan for conducting future team meetings. Write the action plan down and distribute it. Use it for future review.

5. Schedule five to fifteen minutes at the end of the next few meetings to discuss what worked and what didn't about the meeting. Then agree on changes for future meetings. Adjust the meeting action plan as needed.

Tool 9: Assessing Overall Team Effectiveness

In addition to evaluating team meetings, the leader or team members may want to take time to evaluate team effectiveness. This process can be led by the team leader, a well-respected and trusted member, or a neutral facilitator. Teams with limited financial resources may want to lead this process themselves. A team may choose a facilitator who is not attached to the team when trust is low and members worry that another member would not be impartial.

Once you have decided who will lead the evaluation, take the following steps:

1. Schedule a specific team meeting to discuss overall team strengths and areas for improvement.

2. Ask team members to prepare for this meeting by individually completing and returning to the team leader or facilitator Worksheet D: Improving Overall Team Effectiveness (page 59).

3. Combine all the responses onto a single summary worksheet.

4. Give copies of the composite worksheet to team members to assist them in discussion and overall assessment of the team. Celebrate team strengths and address areas for improvement with specific plans or a change in ground rules.

5. Periodically revisit your plans or reassess using the worksheet to check progress at a later date established by the team.

Tool 10: Resolving Conflict within a Team

Conflict is often defined as two or more people having needs and interests that appear to be incompatible.

Conflict can elicit dynamic exchanges that sound like tense and uncomfortable conversations but yield highly productive results. Members must acknowledge the conflict and involve others in cooperative problem-solving efforts. The more quickly one acts, the better chance one has of converting the energy generated by the anger, frustration, and confusion associated with conflict into a positive result.

Conflict is almost inevitable in any team and in fact is a healthy sign that members are committed to and are thinking deeply about the team's work. Work pressures, personality differences and styles, and differences in expectations all may be factors that contribute to conflict between team members.

Interpersonal conflicts are those that occur between two or more team members and are usually related to behavior style, individual history, and cultural differences that affect personal expression. These are best dealt with outside of a team meeting, but this is not always possible. *Team conflicts* more directly affect the whole team, even if only a few members seem to be directly in conflict. Such conflicts often focus on procedures, schedules, strategy choice, resource use, goal and role clarity, or dominant members or factions.

Effective teams are open systems—in other words, a change in any part affects the whole. Therefore, conflict in a small group usually affects everyone and becomes everyone's problem. If all of this sounds familiar, it should. Conflict in a team is a lot like conflict in a family.

People in teams usually behave in one of three ways when they are frustrated with the team's activities or direction: fighting, "flight-ing," and submitting.

Fighting in this context refers to conversational, not physical, fighting—through arguments, for example. Fighting within the team is usually a positive thing, because then the conflict can surface, increasing the potential for resolution.

Flight-ing is people "checking out" mentally, not showing up for meetings, or not completing between-meeting assignments. If demonstrated by one member, this behavior should be addressed outside of the team meeting context. It may be an indication of a personal problem that may require a private conversation. On the other hand, the person may have a work-related conflict that is preventing him or her from giving the team his or her full participation.

Submitting behavior is when members "stay and quit." They participate, but can be heard saying, "Sure, whatever you want." This often indicates that they think their opinion isn't respected or they have tried to be influential and have been unsuccessful. If one team member is behaving this way, discuss it outside of the team context. If a number of people seem to be feeling this way, you might want to discuss it during a team meeting to find out what is causing these feelings.

Following is a process to help your team resolve a conflict.

How to help a team in conflict

1. First, acknowledge the conflict and suggest a cooperative approach to resolving it, referring to the team's ground rules or norms related to conflict, if they exist.

     For example, you could say, "I've noticed several members seem to be making defensive and sarcastic remarks to each other during team meetings. I'd like it if we could openly air any concerns and see if we can cooperatively pinpoint the problems and find solutions."

2. Discuss the impact of the conflict on team performance.

     To continue the example, you could say, "It seems as though these comments are producing a negative tone in our team meetings."

3. Ask team members to identify and discuss the issues around which the conflict was created.

     You could say, "Lee, would you take a minute and let us know what's on your mind? Pat, would you do the same when Lee is done? Any comments or observations from other team members?"

4. As a team, develop alternative approaches or options to address the conflict.

     After hearing about the problem from several team members, you could say, "What are ways we could address this as a team? Let's discuss several possible approaches before we settle on one."

5. As a team, select the best solution and then agree to support the solution.

     You could say, "After listening to all of you, it appears that most people think we should do _____, and then revise our ground rules to reflect that. Have I sized up the options accurately?"

6. Identify future check-in and review points to determine how the solution is working.

   You could start this discussion by saying, "Remember our meeting last month when we talked about _____? How is our solution working?"

7. Thank the team and express confidence in the team's ability to work together and manage their conflicts.

   For example, "I appreciate how this team jumps on the difficult issues that arise and openly discusses them. Thank you."

Tool 11: Managing Conflict between Two Teams

Typically, conflict occurs between teams when they compete for limited resources or when members misunderstand each other. Resources can be human, financial, and informational. Misunderstandings might stem from personality and cultural clashes, value differences, competition and power, noncompliance with rules and policies, or differences over methods or strategies.

A process to help manage conflict between teams

A third-party facilitator or a team leader or member who can remain neutral and objective should lead the following process. The decision to use a facilitator and the process of selecting one should be agreed to by members or representatives of each team. If the team members do not believe the facilitator can remain neutral and objective, an alternative leader should be selected.

1. Team leaders or key members from each team meet together to acknowledge the conflict and to discuss whether it can be resolved.

2. People should divide up into their own teams and each team should develop a list of the attitudes, behaviors, and perceptions it holds about the other team. The list should include positives, negatives, and guesses about what might be on the other team's list.

3. The teams convene and the members or member representative explain their team's list. Clarifying questions are allowed from the other team, but not challenges to the list.

4. Separately and privately, each team then reacts to the other team's list and their own list and develops a list of priority issues that needs to be addressed or resolved with the other team.

   Teams should strive to list these priorities *neutrally*. For instance, you would not want to write, "The other team is rude and leaves our work space really messy." Instead, describe the issue as, "We need to agree on how neat the work space should be when the other team is done."

5. The teams reconvene to share priority lists and develop a single list. Each team commits to resolve the conflicts.

6. Finally, the teams discuss possible resolutions and actions and agree to next steps, timelines, responsibilities, and a way to monitor progress.

7. Team leaders (or their appointees) make sure that the terms of the agreement are carried out.

This process is time consuming and can be emotionally draining and difficult. Consider the extent and depth of the conflict and decide if it should be a half-day meeting, a day-long meeting, or several shorter meetings spread out over time.

Tool 12: Clarifying Roles and Responsibilities

Role confusion simply means that members are confused as to what their membership represents, why they are on the team, or what others expect of them. In multi-organizational groups, such as collaborations, community task forces, multidisciplinary teams, or cross-departmental teams, roles are often less confusing because people presume they are representing their department, neighborhood, or area of expertise. But teams within single departments or teams with significant overlap of expertise may be more likely to experience role confusion.

Symptoms of role and responsibility confusion include members doing the same tasks, work falling between the cracks, missed deadlines, or miscommunication about key events and activities.

A process for clarifying team roles and responsibilities

1. During a team meeting, ask members to individually prepare responses to the following questions:

    a) What is your role on this team?

    b) What should other team members know about your job that would help them do their work?

    c) What do you need from others on the team?

    d) What difficulties or concerns have you had with other members' roles and responsibilities?

    e) What suggestions do you have for changes in structure, assignments, or procedures that would help you do your job more effectively or would improve the team's functioning?

2. Go around the group and ask each person to discuss (a) and (b) above. Differences should be clarified.

3. Continue by asking each person to discuss (c) and (d) above. Encourage good listening skills and understanding, not blaming.

4. Finally, ask each person to share (e) above. Ask the team to respond to (and adopt, if possible) suggestions for change.

Tool 13: Dealing with a Team Member Who Doesn't Follow Through

In teamwork, where the whole of the team relies on individual accountability, performance problems can wreak havoc. Often one person's failure to follow through impacts the progress the rest of the team makes on its goals and plans.

When an individual's failure to follow through is confined to the team's work, people prefer that the individual be addressed by the team leader or another team member. If the performance has not improved after several attempts by the team leader and becomes a pattern of behavior, the person's direct supervisor should be informed and asked to deal with the situation.

How to address a team member's failure to follow through

1. Describe the problem situation objectively; that is, describe the behavior. What is happening that you think should not be happening? Avoid assigning motives, guessing at intentions, or labeling attitudes or values. Use neutral or descriptive terms.

   The trick is naming the behavior, consequences, or subjects at issue without characterizing them. Don't say, "You are inconsiderate," even if you feel that way. Remember, you are confronting the *behavior*, not the person's personality attributes or style.

   You might say, "Pat, you volunteered at the onset of our team project to contact the African American Affairs Council and recommend our next steps on this issue. Based on your status report earlier today, you said you haven't gotten a start on this task yet. I'm concerned about this."

2. Ask the other person for his or her understanding of the situation. Listen carefully, clarify, restate, and summarize until you are sure you understand. Sometimes the person gives you valuable information about the task, the performance problem, or volunteers other information that helps you understand his or her situation.

3. Talk about why you feel it is important to resolve the situation. You could explain the impact the poor performance is having on the team's progress.

   Continuing the earlier example, you could say, "Without input from the African American Affairs Council, we have to stop work on our next report, which we all agreed we wanted done by September."

4. Ask for ideas to solve the problem. Add one or two of your own ideas, if necessary. Try not to impose your own solutions. People tend to like their own ideas best.

5. Agree on a specific plan, including anything you agreed to do.

6. Set a follow-up date to review progress and, when needed, to update the rest of the team on the above steps taken.

Also, do your best at being sensitive to other ways of dealing with performance problems. Different cultures, habits, and styles result in very different ways of doing things. For example, some people are very direct in making their points and some are much less direct than this process suggests.

While you may follow the general outline presented here, keep in mind that it works best when it's done in a way that makes it possible for the person who is not following through to have a fair opportunity to hear about and do something about the particular problem.

Tool 14: Communicating between Meetings

All team members should strive to maintain communications between meetings, team events, or other get-togethers. Formal meetings are often insufficient for all the interaction members need to accomplish their own work.

Here are some tips for communicating between meetings:

- Develop a team membership list with names, jobs, e-mail addresses, fax numbers, addresses, phone numbers, and so forth. Have one person be in charge of maintaining a current team roster.

- Use all available means of communicating. If people have e-mail, decide what can and should be e-mailed. Likewise, determine what subjects or communications should be voice-mailed and what communications should be in person. If electronic bulletin boards are an option, decide how and when to use those to post progress and questions.

- Agree on and publish the priority of the method of communication. For example, in-person contact may be reserved for highest priority, then voice-mail, then e-mail. Some teams have even invented codes to prioritize e-mail communications: *read today, read this week, read before regular team meeting*, and so forth.

- Encourage people not to wait until the next meeting to let others know about progress or problems. As a leader, do not assume members who are just getting to know each other will spontaneously give each other status reports and communicate reliably.

- Encourage team members to communicate directly with each other rather than follow some chain of command.

- Decide who needs to communicate with whom between meetings and how the communication should take place. This reduces time spent at formal meetings and helps prevent misunderstandings. It also helps make sure the right people are informed.

- Have a section of team meeting minutes that includes *action to be taken.* Assign lead responsibilities for each action. Encourage people to use this list as a reminder of the tasks they are accountable for.

- Encourage everyone to read meeting agendas before attending meetings and meeting minutes after meetings. Encourage additional inputs and changes to meeting agendas before the meetings take place.

- Encourage informal conversations in hallways, elevators, around the water cooler, and so forth.

Teamwork Is No Small Miracle!

TEAMWORK—starting a team and keeping it growing—is no small miracle. It's a challenge to pull together many different personalities and accomplish a worthy goal. In today's nonprofit, where people from diverse backgrounds come together, the challenge can be great—but greatly rewarding too.

In these days of fast deadlines and shrinking resources, we need everyone's energy to maintain the motivation and commitment that make teamwork productive and fun. We hope these tools help you water the garden and tend the roots so your team keeps growing.

Appendix

Worksheets

Use the following worksheet for team brainstorming or to prepare for a mission-setting meeting.

a. What *products, services, results,* and *outcomes* do we provide or expect? How do we meet the needs of our clients?

b. Who are the *audiences, customers, clients,* or *stakeholders* of our team? Who are the people we serve, those who serve us, and those who have a stake in our future?

(continued)

c. What *needs* or *functions* does our team serve? What basic issues does our team address in the community or with clients?

d. What *values* (what is important to us?) or *quality standards* (how well? how fast? how carefully?) underlie our work as a team?

Next steps

1. Combine the core points from the collective responses of your team members into a paragraph or two for your team.

2. Develop one or more draft mission statements for the rest of the team to review.

3. Choose the statement that works for everyone.

4. Draft a final mission statement and finalize it with the team's approval.

5. Communicate the mission statement to key stakeholders and others as appropriate.

Step 1

What are some ground rules on which our team needs to agree? *Each* member of the team should write one or two ground rules he or she feels are important to the team below.

Examples:

- *Meetings will start and stop on time.*
- *Members should let others know if they are offended.*
- *Minutes will be taken during meetings and distributed within one week.*

Possible ground rules:

Step 2

Now each person should read his or her answers to Step 1. As each person speaks, write his or her response here or on a flip chart or blackboard so all can see. Write down what people say exactly as they said it.

1.

2.

3.

4.

5.

(continued)

6.

7.

8.

9.

10.

11.

Step 3

As a team, discuss the entire list, combining, eliminating, and modifying ideas as the group wishes. Vote or reach consensus on the ones the team wants to adopt as ground rules. Make a final list, distribute it to all members, and use the ground rules as guidelines for conducting team meetings and working together as a team.

Assess the effectiveness of your team meetings by rating the following:

1. Participation

1	2	3	4	5	6	7

A few dominate,
most quiet

All get their say

2. Objectives of meeting

1	2	3	4	5	6	7

Confusing, diverse

Clear

3. Listening

1	2	3	4	5	6	7

Poor, side conversations,
topic jumping

Good,
all listening

4. Decision making

1	2	3	4	5	6	7

Decisions avoided,
a few members dominate

Good decisions are
made and are supported

5. Expression of feelings

1	2	3	4	5	6	7

Closed, withholding,
fearful, low trust

Open and
frank discussions

6. Conflict

1	2	3	4	5	6	7

Suppressed,
ignored, tension

Expressed, dealt
with constructively

7. Action

1	2	3	4	5	6	7

Not clear what's
going to happen

Desired actions clear,
items accomplished

8. Responsibility for effective meetings

1	2	3	4	5	6	7

Leader on own,
few others care

Everyone helps to
keep us on track

Rate your team effectiveness using the following rating scale:

1=strongly disagree   2=disagree   3=not sure or neutral   4=agree   5=strongly agree

Use the space below each statement to explain your answer.

1. We understand our team's goals and mission.   1 2 3 4 5

2. We are committed to our team's goals and mission.   1 2 3 4 5

3. Our goals and mission are worthwhile and challenging.   1 2 3 4 5

4. Everyone understands everyone else's roles and responsibilities. 1 2 3 4 5

5. We agree on each other's roles and responsibilities.   1 2 3 4 5

(continued)

1=strongly disagree   2=disagree   3=not sure or neutral   4=agree   5=strongly agree

6. Our procedures are clear and help us accomplish our work as a team.   1   2   3   4   5

7. Our procedures are respected and followed.   1   2   3   4   5

8. We have effective working relationships on this team.   1   2   3   4   5

9. Our team does a good job of resolving conflict.   1   2   3   4   5

10. We openly give and ask for feedback from each other.   1   2   3   4   5

11. We have a trusting and respectful work environment on our team.   1   2   3   4   5

1=strongly disagree   2=disagree   3=not sure or neutral   4=agree   5=strongly agree

12. We reward ourselves as a team and celebrate our accomplishments.   1   2   3   4   5

13. Our team leader(s) is a positive role model.   1   2   3   4   5

14. Our team leader(s) helps create a positive atmosphere when we   1   2   3   4   5
     work together and during team meetings.

15. Our team leader(s) shares power and encourages the most   1   2   3   4   5
     competent to lead.

16. Our team leader(s) ensures we have productive meetings.   1   2   3   4   5

(continued)

List three *strengths* of the team and how each strength helps the team.

1.

2.

3.

List three *areas for improvement or change* and your suggestions for bringing about these changes or improvements.

1.

2.

3.

List three *things you need from others on this team* that would help you be more effective.

1.

2.

3.

Annotated References

Conger, Jay. *The Charismatic Leader.* San Francisco, CA: Jossey-Bass, 1989.

> Conger's book explains how the charismatic leader's qualities of creativity, inspiration, unconventionality, vision, and risk-taking can help bring about effective change in organizations damaged by long periods of inertia. The author's combination of research, inspiring examples, and advice makes for a friendly read.

Dyer, William. *Team Building: Issues and Alternatives.* Reading, MA: Addison Wesley, 1987.

> While this book was published more than a decade ago, it is excellent for the leader or facilitator who wants to plan and implement serious team building. It covers diagnosing problems, planning and designing a team-building program, addressing conflict in an ongoing team, revitalizing the complacent team, and reducing inter-team conflict.

Harper, Ann, and Bob Harper. *Succeeding as a Self-Directed Work Team* (1991) and *Skill Building for Self-Directed Team Members* (1992). New York: MW Corporation.

> The books by these authors are both practical how-to guides. *Succeeding as a Self-Directed Work Team* uses a question-and-answer format and is appropriate to buy and hand out to team members. Questions include "What is a self-directed work team and how is it different from

traditional work?"; "What different attitudes are required?"; and "What are the key elements of high-performing teams?"

Skill Building for Self-Directed Team Members consists of worksheets, readings, checklists, assessments on communications, services, change, motivations, feedback, conflict, and other skills needed for teamwork.

Katzenbach, John R., and Douglas K. Smith. *The Wisdom of Teams: Creating the High Performance Organization*. New York: McKinsey and Company, 1993.

This book describes the basics of team effectiveness, but gives extra attention to the team performance curve (the stages of team development) and how to keep a team performing at its peak potential in each stage. An excellent resource for project team leaders and members who want to enhance team performance and productivity.

Shonk, James H. *Team-Based Organizations: Developing a Successful Team Environment*. Homewood, IL: Business One Irwin, 1992.

This book helps leaders learn how to restructure their organizations into team-based organizations. Topics outlined include key decisions to make, whether teams are right for your organization, types of teams, how to get started, how to design the structure, what training is critical, and the shift in leadership roles and responsibilities.

Varney, Glenn H. *Building Productive Teams: An Action Guide and Resource Book*. San Francisco, CA: Jossey-Bass, 1989.

This 138-page book is full of practical lists, tips, and processes for recognizing unproductive teams, diagnosing problems, action planning, defining roles, setting goals, making decisions, and leading teams effectively. Varney has several other books available if you like his style.

Collaboration Handbook: Creating, Sustaining, and Enjoying the Journey

by Michael Winer and Karen Ray

Shows you how to get a collaboration going, set goals, determine everyone's roles, create an action plan, and evaluate the results. Includes a case study of one collaboration from start to finish, helpful tips on how to avoid pitfalls, and worksheets to keep everyone on track.

192 pages, softcover, $28.00

Collaboration: What Makes It Work

by Wilder Research Center

An in-depth review of current collaboration research. Major findings are summarized, critical conclusions are drawn, and nineteen key factors influencing successful collaborations are identified. See if your collaboration's plans include the necessary ingredients.

53 pages, softcover, $14.00

Community Building: What Makes It Work

by Wilder Research Center

Shows you what really does (and doesn't) contribute to community building success. Reveals twenty-eight keys to help you build community more effectively. Includes detailed descriptions of each factor, case examples of how they play out, and practical questions to assess your work.

112 pages, softcover, $20.00

Consulting with Nonprofits: A Practitioner's Guide

by Carol A. Lukas

A step-by-step, comprehensive guide for consultants. Addresses the art of consulting, how to run your business, and much more. Also includes tips and anecdotes from thirty skilled consultants.

240 pages, softcover, $35.00

Coping with Cutbacks: The Nonprofit Guide to Success When Times Are Tight

by Emil Angelica and Vincent Hyman

Devolution—the delegation of power from the federal government to local governments—means BIG changes for nonprofits, including far less government funding. This guide provides a process for finding creative ways to meet your mission goals by expanding and deepening your nonprofit's connection to the community. Also includes 180 cutback strategies you can put to use right away. Your organization doesn't have to be in a financial crisis in order to benefit from this book.

128 pages, softcover, $20.00

Marketing Workbook for Nonprofit Organizations Volume I: Develop the Plan

by Gary J. Stern

Don't just wish for results—get them! Here's how to create a straightforward, usable marketing plan. Includes the six P's of Marketing, how to use them effectively, a sample marketing plan, and detachable worksheets.

132 pages, softcover, $25.00

To order see order form or call TOLL-FREE 1-800-274-6024

Marketing Workbook for Nonprofit Organizations Volume II: Mobilize People for Marketing Success

by Gary J. Stern

Put together a successful promotional campaign based on the most persuasive tool of all: personal contact. Learn how to mobilize your entire organization, its staff, volunteers, and supporters in a focused, one-to-one marketing campaign. Provides step-by-step instructions, sample agendas for motivational trainings, and worksheets to keep the campaign organized and on track. Also includes *Pocket Guide for Marketing Representatives.* In it, your marketing representatives can record key campaign messages and find motivational reminders.

192 pages, softcover, $25.00

Strategic Planning Workbook for Nonprofit Organizations, Revised and Updated

by Bryan Barry

Chart a wise course for your nonprofit's future. This time-tested workbook gives you practical step-by-step guidance, real-life examples, one nonprofit's complete strategic plan, and easy-to-use worksheets.

144 pages, softcover, $25.00

From the Wilder Nonprofit Field Guide Series

Conducting Successful Focus Groups

by Judith Sharken Simon

Shows you how to collect valuable information without a lot of money or special expertise. Using this proven technique, you'll get essential opinions and feedback to help you check out your assumptions, do better strategic planning, improve services or products, build goodwill, and more.

80 pages, softcover, $15.00

Getting Started on the Internet

by Gary M. Grobman and Gary B. Grant

If all that's standing between you and the internet is a little fear, lack of know-how, or both, this concise guide will help you quickly get connected to the world's largest library. This guide also shows you how to use the internet to uncover valuable information and help your nonprofit be more productive.

64 pages, softcover, $15.00

Fundraising on the Internet

by Gary M. Grobman, Gary B. Grant, and Steve Roller

Your quick road map to using the internet as a new fundraising channel. Whether you want to attract new donors, troll for grants, or get listed on sites that assist donors, this practical guide will help. Even if you don't intend to raise a dime on the internet, this book will show you how to use the internet to learn more about the art of fundraising.

Also includes detailed reviews of 77 web sites useful to fundraisers, including foundations, charities, prospect research sites, and sites that assist donors.

64 pages, softcover, $15.00

Violence Prevention and Intervention Titles

The Little Book of Peace

Designed and illustrated by Kelly O. Finnerty

A pocket-size guide to help people think about violence and talk about it with their families and friends. Over 250,000 copies of this booklet are in use in schools, homes, churches, businesses, and prisons. You may download a free copy of *The Little Book of Peace* from our web site at www.wilder.org.

24 pages, $.65 each (minimum order 10 copies)

Journey Beyond Abuse
A Step-by-Step Guide to Facilitating Women's Domestic Abuse Groups

by Kay-Laurel Fischer, MA, LP and Michael F. McGrane, LICSW

Create a program where women increase their understanding of the dynamics of abuse, feel less alone and isolated, and have a greater awareness of channels to safety. This book provides complete tools for facilitating effective groups. It includes twenty-one group activities that you can combine to create groups of differing length and focus. Also gives you tips on how to handle twenty-eight special issues such as child care, safety and protection, and substance abuse, plus much more.

208 pages, softcover, $45.00

Moving Beyond Abuse
Stories and Questions for Women Who Have Lived with Abuse

(Companion guided journal to Journey Beyond Abuse)

A series of stories and questions that coordinate with the sessions provided in the facilitator's guide. This journal can be used in coordination with a women's group or with the guidance of a counselor in other forms of support for dealing with abuse issues. The open-ended questions provide gentle direction toward gaining insights that help affirm inner strength and heal the wounds of abuse.

88 pages, softcover, $10.00

Foundations for Violence-Free Living
A Step-by-Step Guide to Facilitating Men's Domestic Abuse Groups

by David J. Mathews, MA, LICSW

A complete guide to facilitating a men's domestic abuse program. Includes twenty-nine activities, detailed guidelines for presenting each activity, and a discussion of psychological issues that may arise out of each activity. Also gives you tips for intake, individual counseling, facilitating groups, working with resistant clients, and recommended policies and releases.

240 pages, softcover, $45.00

On the Level

(Participant's workbook to Foundations for Violence-Free Living)

Contains forty-nine worksheets including midterm and final evaluations. Men can record their insights and progress. A permanent binding makes the workbook easy to carry home for outside assignments, and you don't have to make any trips to the copy machine.

160 pages, softcover, $15.00

What Works in Preventing Rural Violence

by Wilder Research Center

An in-depth review of eighty-eight effective strategies you can use to prevent and intervene in violent behaviors, improve services for victims, and reduce repeat offenses. Strategies are organized into seven categories—assaultive violence, child abuse, rape and sexual assault, domestic abuse, elder abuse, suicide, and bias (hate) crimes. This report also includes a Community Report Card with step-by-step directions on how you can collect, record, and use information about violence in your community.

94 pages, softcover, $17.00

Five Easy Ways to Order

 Call toll-free: **1-800-274-6024**

 Fax: 651-642-2061

 Mail: Amherst H. Wilder Foundation
PO Box 2029
Danbury, CT 06813-2029

E-mail: books@wilder.org
On-line: www.wilder.org

OUR NO-RISK GUARANTEE

If you aren't completely satisfied with any book,
simply send it back within 30 days for a full refund.

Save when you order in quantity

We offer substantial discounts on orders of ten or more copies
of any single title. Please call for details.

Visit our web site at www.wilder.org

Detailed information on all of our publications—such as table
of contents and discounts—is on our web site.

Send us your manuscript

Wilder Publishing Center continually seeks manuscripts and
proposals for publications in the fields of nonprofit management and community development. Send us your proposal or
manuscript. Or, for more information, call us at 651-659-6024
and ask for our author guidelines or download them from our
web site.

Order Form

Prices subject to change

	QTY.	PRICE EACH	TOTAL AMOUNT
Collaboration Handbook: Creating, Sustaining, and Enjoying the Journey		$28.00	
Collaboration: What Makes It Work		14.00	
Community Building: What Makes It Work		20.00	
Consulting with Nonprofits: A Practitioner's Guide		35.00	
Coping with Cutbacks: The Nonprofit Guide to Success When Times Are Tight		20.00	
Foundations for Violence-Free Living (facilitator's guide)		45.00	
On the Level (participant's workbook to Foundation's for Violence-Free Living)		15.00	
Journey Beyond Abuse (facilitator's guide)		45.00	
Moving Beyond Abuse (participant's journal)		10.00	
The Little Book of Peace (minimum order 10 copies)		0.65	
Marketing Workbook for Nonprofit Organizations Vol. I: Develop the Plan		25.00	
Marketing Workbook for Nonprofit Organizations Vol. II: Mobilize People for Marketing Success		25.00	
Pocket Guide for Marketing Representatives (1 copy free with order of Marketing Vol. II)		1.95	
Strategic Planning Workbook for Nonprofit Organizations, Revised and Updated		25.00	
What Works in Preventing Rural Violence		17.00	
The Wilder Nonprofit Field Guide to Conducting Successful Focus Groups		15.00	
The Wilder Nonprofit Field Guide to Developing Effective Teams		15.00	
The Wilder Nonprofit Field Guide to Fundraising on the Internet		15.00	
The Wilder Nonprofit Field Guide to Getting Started on the Internet		15.00	
		SUBTOTAL	
In MN, add 7% sales tax or attach exempt cert.			
		SHIPPING	
		TOTAL	

Send to (please print or attach business card)

Name _____

Organization _____

Address _____

_____

City _____ State _____ ZIP _____

Phone *(in case we have questions)* (_____) _____

Payment Method VISA MasterCard AMERICAN EXPRESS Cards

Card # _____

Expiration Date _____

Signature (required) _____

☐ Check/Money Order (payable to A. H. Wilder Foundation)

☐ Bill Me (for orders under $100) PO # _____

Shipping & Handling

If order totals: ***Add:***

Up to $30.00 $4.00

$30.01 - 60.00 $5.00

$60.01 - 150.00 $6.00

$150.01 - 500.00 $8.00

Over $500.00 3% of order

Outside the U.S. or Canada, add an addtl. U.S. $5.00.

• Please allow two weeks for delivery.

• Special RUSH delivery is available—call for rates.

We occasionally make our mailing list available to carefully selected companies. If you do not wish to have your name included, please check here ☐

Mail orders to: Amherst H. Wilder Foundation • PO Box 2029 • Danbury, CT • 06813-2029 • 1-800-274-6024